THE ARAB SPRING

BY VALERIE BODDEN

CREATIVE EDUCATION • CREATIVE PAPERBACKS

Published by Creative Education and Creative Paperbacks
P.O. Box 227, Mankato, Minnesota 56002
Creative Education and Creative Paperbacks are imprints of
The Creative Company
www.thecreativecompany.us

Design and production by The Design Lab
Art direction by Rita Marshall
Printed in the United States of America

Photographs by Corbis (YAHYA ARHAB/epa, ZOHRA BENSEMRA/Reuters,
AMR ABDALLAH DALSH/Reuters, MOHAMED ABD EL GHANY/Reuters,
Richard Levine/Demotix, MOHAMED MESSARA/epa, MirakHikimori/Demotix,
Amr Nabil/AP, Wissam Nassar, Sallie Pisch/Demotix, Louis Quail/In Pictures,
Luke Somers/Demotix, ZOUBEIR SOUISSI/Reuters, STRINGER/Reuters, Hamza
Turkia/Xinhua Press), Creative Commons Wikimedia (Jesse B. Awalt, Chatham
House, Marc Müller/MSC, PHGCOM, Presidenza della Repubblica), Design
Lab, Dreamstime (Thomas Dutour, Mohamed Elsayyed, Richard Gunion),
Shutterstock (thomas koch)

Library of Congress Cataloging in Publication
Bodden, Valerie.
The Arab spring / Valerie Bodden.
p. cm. — (Turning points)
Includes bibliographical references and index.
Summary: A historical account of the Arab Spring, includ
up to the string of protests, the people involved, the condi
instability, and the lingering aftermath.

ISBN 978-1-60818-745-4 (hardcover)
ISBN 978-1-62832-341-2 (pbk)
ISBN 978-1-56660-780-3 (eBook)
Arab Spring, 2010—Juvenile literature.

JQ1850.A91 B63 2016
909/.097492708312—dc23   2016002681

CCSS: RI.5.1, 2, 3, 8; RI. 6.1, 2, 4, 7; RH.6-8.3, 4, 5, 6, 7

First Edition HC 9 8 7 6 5 4 3 2 1
First Edition PBK 9 8 7 6 5 4 3 2 1

Cover, main image: Anti-Qaddafi graffiti is seen in Tripoli,

TABLE *of* CONTENTS

No one saw it coming. That's what world leaders, political scientists, and scholars would say in the weeks and months following the outbreak of the Arab Spring. This revolution was a massive move to overthrow **dictators** throughout the Arab world of North Africa and the Middle East. It began in Tunisia in December 2010. Peaceful protesters there overthrew longtime dictator Zine el-Abidine Ben Ali. People across the Middle East watched events unfold on social media and satellite television. Soon, nearly the entire Arab world swarmed with protesters inspired by Tunisia's example.

On November 11, 2011, protesters gathered in Cairo's Tahrir Square to demonstrate against oppressive leadership.

Some of the protests remained peaceful. But others were met with violence. Some sparked civil wars that lasted for months or years. A few countries were able to repeat Tunisia's success in overthrowing their governments. But even then, new, **democratic** governments struggled to get off the ground. Many countries soon fell back into violence and repression. Meanwhile, world leaders struggled to come up with a response. And new threats, such as the so-called Islamic State, arose from the chaos. By 2015, only Tunisia was able to celebrate a successful revolution. The rest of the Middle East remained unsettled. The outcome of this turning point in history remains to be seen.

IRELAND U. K. NETH. POLAND BELARUS

GERMANY CZECH UKRAINE KAZAKHST

BELGIUM LUX. SLOVAKIA MOLDOVA

FRANCE SWITZ. AUSTRIA HUNGARY ROMANIA UZBEKISTAN

ITALY SLOVENIA CROATIA YUGOSLAVIA BULGARIA GEORGIA

PORTUGAL BOSNIA MACEDONIA ARMENIA AZERBAIJAN TURKMENISTAN

SPAIN GREECE ALBANIA TURKEY AFGHANIST

NORTH CYPRUS IRAN PAKIS

Canary Islands CYPRUS SYRIA

★Algiers ★Tunis LEBANON Baghdad ★

★Rabat TUNISIA Tripoli ISRAEL IRAQ

MOROCCO JORDAN KUWAIT

ALGERIA Cairo ★ BAHRAIN

WESTERN LIBYA EGYPT Riyadh QATAR

SAHARA ★ U. A. E. ★Muscat

(occupied by Morocco) SAUDI ARABIA OMAN

MAURITANIA SUDAN YEMEN

★Nouakchott MALI NIGER Khartoum ERITREA ★Sanaa

SENEGAL ★ DJIBOUTI

GAMBIA CHAD SOMALIA

GUINEA BISSAU BURKINA FASO NIGERIA

GUINEA GHANA BENIN CENTRAL AFRICAN SOUTH SUDAN ETHIOPIA

SIERRA LEONE COTE TOGO REPUBLIC ★Mogadishu

D'IVOIRE CAMEROON

LIBERIA EQUATORIAL GUINEA UGANDA KENYA

SAO TOME & PRINCIPE CONGO

ATLANTIC GABON DEM. REP. RWANDA

OF CONGO BURUND

ANGOLA TANZANIA COMOROS

OCEAN ZAMBIA MALAWI

ANGOLA ZIMBABWE MOZAMBIQUE

NAMIBIA BOTSWANA MADAGASCAR

SWAZILAND

*Nearly every country in the
Arab world has participated
in or been affected by events
of the Arab Spring.*

SOUTH AFRICA LESOTHO

INDIA

CHAPTER ONE

LIFE OF REPRESSION

The Arab world is made up of 22 countries: Algeria, Bahrain, Comoros, Djibouti, Egypt, Iraq, Jordan, Kuwait, Lebanon, Libya, Mauritania, Morocco, Oman, Qatar, the Palestinian territories, Saudi Arabia, Somalia, Sudan, Syria, Tunisia, the United Arab Emirates, and Yemen. The Arab people are connected by a shared language (Arabic), culture, and history. The majority of Arabs are Muslim. But conflict between the religion's Sunni and Shia sects divides much of the Middle East. About 85 to 90 percent of Muslims belong to the more orthodox, or traditional, Sunni sect. Shia make up a minority of the Muslim population. But large numbers of Shia live in Iraq, Bahrain, Yemen, Kuwait, Lebanon, Qatar, Syria, Saudi Arabia, and the United Arab Emirates. Many Shia also live in the non-Arab countries of the Middle East, such as Iran.

The Arab world has a long history. The peoples of North Africa and the Middle East were once among the most advanced civilizations of their time. But in the early centuries A.D., they were conquered by the Roman Empire. From the early 600s to the mid-1200s, Arab **dynasties** ruled

Coin from Arab dynasty 661–750 A.D.

Protesters in Tunisia marched against media censorship as well as the oppression of their right to free speech.

the region. But they were overtaken by the **Ottoman Empire**, which fell apart after World War I. In its place, European powers such as Great Britain and France divided the Arab world among themselves as colonies. It was not until after World War II that most Middle Eastern countries became independent. But independence did not always bring better living conditions. Most countries struggled to find stability as leader after leader was forced out in military **coups**.

Eventually, many Arab countries came to be ruled by ruthless dictators who remained in power for decades. By 2011, Libya's president Muammar Gaddafi had ruled for 42 years. The Assad family had headed Syria for 41 years. In Yemen, Ali Abdullah Saleh had been president for 33 years. Egyptian president Hosni Mubarak held onto his 30-year rule through fraudulent elections. And Tunisia's Ben Ali used sham elections to retain power for 24 years.

Such dictators made citizens of Arab countries among the least free in the world. In many countries, they could not form political parties to run in elections. Citizens could not criticize the government for fear of being jailed. In Egypt, anyone suspected of a crime could be hauled to the police station to be beaten or tortured. Those suspected of acting against the **regime** might be held for years without trial. In Libya and Syria, too, those who opposed the regime were often arrested or tortured.

Middle Eastern governments also tightly controlled and **censored** the media. This ensured that the regimes would be shown only in a positive light. In some countries, such as Tunisia, censorship reached to political websites and YouTube. In Bahrain, bloggers and journalists who opposed the regime faced arrest.

The situation in the Middle East worsened when a financial crisis rocked the world in 2008. Most countries in this region depend heavily on food **imports**. As the cost of wheat and other foods shot up, families had to spend up to 63 percent of their income just to eat. (In comparison, families in the United States generally spend about 7 percent of their income on food.)

Despite such conditions, many people in the Middle East were well educated. Tunisia had passed a law in 1991 requiring all children to attend school. In Libya, the literacy rate reached 100 percent among 15- to 24-year-olds. Thriving universities educated masses of young adults in many Arab countries.

But when those young adults graduated from college, many faced difficulties in finding jobs. The sheer number of young people was one problem. In most Arab countries, 30 percent of the population was between the ages of 15 and 29. But only a limited number of jobs were available to those with college degrees. By 2010, college graduates made up a large percentage of the unemployed in the Middle

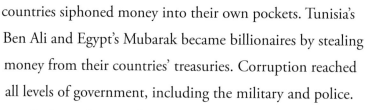

East. Many expected to spend four years or more looking for a job. With no jobs to support themselves, graduates often felt helpless to marry and start a family.

While their citizens struggled to find work and food, the leaders of many countries siphoned money into their own pockets. Tunisia's Ben Ali and Egypt's Mubarak became billionaires by stealing money from their countries' treasuries. Corruption reached all levels of government, including the military and police.

Hosni Mubarak

Such conditions often led people to take to the streets despite the threat of punishment. Throughout the early 2000s, citizens in Egypt, Jordan, Kuwait, Tunisia, Algeria, Bahrain, and Yemen protested against poor wages, climbing food prices, and the denial of basic rights. In some cases, protests took the form of peaceful sit-ins. In others, they resulted in street violence. In a few cases, protesters were even bold enough to call for the overthrow of the regime. In Egypt, for example, protesters belonging to the *Kefaya* ("Enough") movement called for Mubarak to step down. In Lebanon, protesters successfully demanded the removal of the Syrian military, which had occupied the country for 30 years. But in most countries, protest movements remained small, and governments easily quashed them.

Still, the sweeping power of the Arab regimes was beginning to erode. In 1996, the Arabic-language news network Al Jazeera had begun broadcasting. Based in Qatar, Al Jazeera was shown throughout the Arab world. It helped foster a feeling of shared identity among Arab peoples with coverage that was often highly critical of Arab regimes.

Activist George Ishak, a cofounder of the Kefaya movement, led many protests against Mubarak in Egypt.

By 2010, many people in the Arab world also had access to the Internet, cell phones, and social media. For years, Arab dictators had relied on tight control of the media. But they had no authority over what appeared online. This made it harder to hide corruption, security crackdowns, and **human rights** violations.

In addition, the Internet allowed Arabs to openly express their frustration with their governments. Social media sites such as Facebook and Twitter soon became forums for political debate among young people. In June

POINTING OUT

SOCIAL MEDIA AND REVOLUTION

Reporting from Cairo on the second day of Egypt's uprising, CNN correspondent Ben Wedeman called it "a very techie revolution." He noted that protesters were "half the time chanting, the other time they're looking down at their mobile phones to read text messages, to check Facebook, to check Twitter." Political scientist Marc Lynch agreed that social media played a huge role in the Arab Spring. But he emphasized, "there were simply not enough Arab users of social media for that alone to have made the difference." Lynch credited Al Jazeera's broadcasts with inspiring Arabs to join the protest movements.

Increased access to cell phones and the Internet enabled Arabs to share experiences and opinions with ease.

After Khaled Said's death, people honored him as a hero who exposed the corruption of Mubarak's police force.

2010, 28-year-old Egyptian businessman Khaled Said was dragged from an Internet café and beaten to death by police. Afterward, cell phone photos of his beaten body were posted to a Facebook page called "We Are All Khaled Said." The page soon had 400,000 followers. It had become another place to vent against the Egyptian government. "I just felt that we are all Khaled Said," said Wael Ghoneim, who helped create the page. "That was a feeling. It wasn't a brand name…. We were all of these young Egyptians who could die and no one [would be] held accountable."

Whatever Bouazizi's intent, he is remembered by some in his Tunisian hometown as a martyr.

THE DOMINOES FALL

On December 17, 2010, 26-year-old Mohamed Bouazizi stood at his fruit cart on a dusty street in Sidi Bouzid, a small city in central Tunisia. Bouazizi had supported his parents and siblings since he was 12 years old. Every day, he scrimped to provide enough food for the family of 8. In a good week, he might earn $75.

Bouazizi was used to police corruption in his city. Police officers had often taken away his cart and stolen his fruit. Today was no different. A police officer grabbed several crates of fruit along with Bouazizi's scales. The young man was left with nothing. When the officer refused to give the items back, Bouazizi went to local officials to complain. But they wouldn't do anything to help. So Bouazizi bought a can of paint thinner, poured it over his body, and lit himself on fire. He died nearly three weeks later, on January 4, 2011.

Bouazizi's family insisted that the young man had had no interest in politics. They said his suicide was simply a reaction to his circumstances. "He never even watched the news," his mother said. "People like Mohamed are concerned with doing business. They don't understand anything about politics." Yet, political scientist Marc Lynch argues there was more to the suicide. "Bouazizi's act of desperation was not the inarticulate expression of rage that it has been portrayed to be," he said. "It was a … political act designed to provoke precisely the kind of popular response it achieved."

Whether purposely political or not, Bouazizi's act set off a revolution. The day after Bouazizi lit himself on fire, the people of his hometown took to the streets. Some posted videos and pictures of the protests on Facebook and YouTube. Journalists at Al Jazeera took notice. Within days, the satellite TV network was broadcasting from the scene. By

POINTING OUT

GIVING VOICE TO THE ARAB WORLD

Unlike most media outlets in the Middle East, the Qatar-based television network Al Jazeera faced little censorship. It became known for political talk shows that weren't afraid to question Arab regimes. According to Ali Hashem, a former Al Jazeera reporter, the network was many Arabs' first contact with dissent. The network showed Arabs "saying in Arabic what they had only dared to say before on Western channels in English or French," Hashem said. Former Al Jazeera director general Wadah Khanfar said the network's role was "liberating the Arab mind. We created the idea in the Arab mind that when you have a right, you should fight for it."

Egypt's 18-day revolution against president Hosni Mubarak resulted in more than 800 deaths.

the end of December, protests had spread to most Tunisian cities. They were largely peaceful, but police forces in various cities are believed to have killed 150 demonstrators.

On January 13, thousands of people crowded into the streets of the Tunisian capital, Tunis. Ben Ali ordered the army to open fire. But the army's leaders refused. Without their support, Ben Ali could do nothing. On January 14, he fled the country. Wild celebrations broke out across Tunisia.

People in other Middle Eastern countries celebrated with the Tunisians—and were inspired by them. "Thank you to the great Tunisian people for proving to the world that the Arab peoples are not dead," Egyptian journalist Ibrahim Eissa wrote. Meanwhile, activists in his country began making plans for their own revolution.

On January 25, 2011, tens of thousands of Egyptians poured into Tahrir Square, a large public area in downtown Cairo. Thousands more rallied in other cities across Egypt. The first day of protests remained largely peaceful. But the next three days were marked by violence as protesters and police forces clashed. On January 28, protesters across the country held a "Day of Rage." They surrounded and burned police stations and prisons. Some openly fought police officers. More than 300 people were killed, and thousands more were injured. The next day, the military announced that it would not fire on

Protesters gathered in front of the White House in 2011 as anti-Mubarak demonstrations spread worldwide.

FREEDOM is CONTAGIOUS
SPREAD The WORD.

demonstrators. On February 11, after 18 days of protests, Mubarak resigned at the insistence of the army.

As they celebrated their victory, some Egyptians urged people in other parts of the Arab world to follow their example. "We are setting a role model for the dictatorships around us," said 39-year-old protester Khalid Shaheen. "Democracy is coming." He seemed to be right, as nearly every Arab country soon teemed with its own revolts.

Even before Egypt's success, thousands of protesters in Yemen were demanding the overthrow of their country's dictator, Ali Abdullah Saleh. The regime responded with violence. But this only spurred more people to take to the streets. In June, Saleh was wounded by a bomb blast in the presidential compound. He was taken to Saudi Arabia for medical treatment. Although he returned to the country briefly in September, by November, he had resigned.

The trend of violence continued and escalated in Libya, where protests broke out on February 15. The government almost immediately resorted to force. Soldiers fired on unarmed protesters in the streets. In response, the protesters seized weapons from a local military post. Over the next weeks, the country declined into civil war. Gaddafi's forces were soon crushing the rebels as the leader proclaimed, "The people who don't love me don't deserve to live." By March, many Arabs were calling for Western help— something Arab nations usually resisted. Members of the **North Atlantic Treaty Organization (NATO)**, including the U.S., began air strikes against Gaddafi's

Muammar Gaddafi

forces. By August, Gaddafi's regime had fallen. He was captured and killed in October. An estimated 30,000 Libyans had died in the 8-month war.

But the bloodiest conflict of the Arab Spring was still to come. At first, it seemed that the unrest would skip Syria, where fear and intimidation generally prevented popular uprisings. Initial attempts to arrange protests in January and February went nowhere. The few people who showed up were easily turned back by security forces. Then, in March 2011, a group of 10 children under the age of 15 were caught writing "Down with the system" on a wall in the city of

POINTING OUT

A REVOLUTION BY ANY OTHER NAME

The term "Arab Spring" is based on the 1968 "Prague Spring," a brief period of freedom in **communist** *Czechoslovakia. But many political observers say that the term does not accurately reflect the situation in the Middle East. For one thing, most of the revolutions in the region began in winter, not spring. In addition, the term "spring" usually implies a sense of renewal. But for the most part, the Arab Spring has not yet brought this to the Middle East. Despite such objections, the term "Arab Spring" seems to have caught on.*

Muammar Gaddafi's death made the front page of newspapers around the world.

Daraa. They were jailed and tortured. Parents and others took to the city's streets, demanding the children's release. Police responded with gunfire, killing three. The killings, in turn, set off uprisings across the country. As rebels armed themselves to fight against Assad's forces, the country fell into civil war.

Meanwhile, protests also broke out in several Middle Eastern **monarchies**, including Jordan, Morocco, Kuwait, Saudi Arabia, and Oman. Compared with protests in other countries, these movements remained relatively small. Most called for reform rather than revolution. And in many cases, the monarchs were quick to offer changes. In Jordan, the king removed hated prime minister Samir al-Rifai. The Moroccan king vowed to make **constitutional** changes. And in Oman, people were promised more jobs and higher salaries.

Protesters were less successful in Bahrain, a small island nation of mostly Shia Muslims ruled by a Sunni king. Protests there began February 14, 2011. At their peak, nearly 500,000 people—half the country's population—flooded the streets. But a month later, troops from neighboring Saudi Arabia were brought in to help put down the revolt. According to Lynch, the country became "one of the first great reversals of the Arab uprisings."

CHAPTER THREE

UNCERTAIN FUTURE

It seemed as though the Arab Spring might finally be paving the way toward democracy in the Middle East. But by April 2011, the spirit of hope and unity that had marked the protests began to fade. Groups that had banded together to overthrow dictators were suddenly arguing over how their newly freed countries would be run.

As of early 2015, Tunisia was the only country to form a true democracy.

Moncef Marzouki

The process took four years. After Ben Ali fled in January 2011, the military took power until elections could be held. In October 2011, Tunisians flocked to the polls to elect a new parliament. The majority of parliamentary seats were won by the Islamist Ennahda Party. Islamists believe that Islam should play a role in the government. But Ennahda members in parliament pledged to establish a secular (non-religious) constitution. They chose Moncef Marzouki to serve as **interim** president. Under his rule, citizens enjoyed new freedoms, such as the ability to openly debate politics. But poverty, unemployment, and corruption were still widespread.

In 2011 and 2014, Tunisia held its first free elections since 1956, setting it on the path to democracy.

The new government also began to enforce Islamic rules. Restaurants and coffee shops were forced to close during the Islamic holy month of **Ramadan**, for example. In August 2013, thousands of demonstrators gathered in Tunis to protest. In response, the government peacefully resigned in January 2014.

Tunisia's first free presidential elections were held in December 2014. They brought 88-year-old Beji Caid Essebsi to power. Not everyone was happy, though. Some worried that Essebsi had ties to the old Ben Ali regime. But the Arabic newspaper *Al Arabiya* commended Tunisia for being "the sole survivor of the Arab Spring." U.S.

POINTING OUT

OFF THE AIR

In February 2015, a new Arab news channel called Alarab was launched in Bahrain. The station's director, Jamal Khashoggi, said the channel would be open to anyone's viewpoint. "We are not going to take sides," he said. "We will provide accurate and objective information." With that in mind, Alarab's first broadcast included an interview with a Bahraini government official as well as one with an anti-government activist. Less than 24 hours later, the Bahraini government pulled the channel off the air. Alarab planned to relocate to Cyprus, Lebanon, or London.

Essebsi supporters flooded Tunisian streets to celebrate his victory over interim president Moncef Marzouki.

POINTING OUT

APOLOGIZING TO A DICTATOR

Not all Arabs sided with Arab Spring protesters. Only days after President Mubarak of Egypt resigned, hundreds of his supporters held their own protest against the revolution. Although some protesters favored change, they felt Mubarak's overthrow was the wrong way to achieve it. "This was very humiliating to the man who served this country for decades," one protester said. Some thought the president should have been given a chance to reform the country before being forced out. In 2012, Mubarak was sentenced to life in prison for his role in the deaths of anti-regime protesters. The sentence was later overturned.

president Barack Obama also praised the Tunisian people for continuing "to inspire people across their region and around the world."

Although the Egyptian revolution had started out much like Tunisia's, its transition period was very different. After Mubarak resigned, military leaders known as the Supreme Council of the Armed Forces (SCAF) took over the government. But conditions in the country did not improve. The economy worsened, and police corruption abounded. Time and again, demonstrators returned to the streets. But they were often forcibly dispersed, jailed, and tortured.

Though it is best known as the site of protests during the Arab Spring, Egypt's Tahrir Square has also hosted joyous celebrations.

Finally, in June 2012, presidential elections were held. They brought Mohamed Morsi, leader of an Islamist group called the Muslim Brotherhood, to power. Within a year, economic conditions in the country had declined even further. In addition, Morsi began to impose Islamic law on the country. Protests again erupted. On July 3, 2013, the army forced the president out and again took over the government. All unofficial demonstrations were banned. Protests held in defiance of the law resulted in hundreds of deaths and arrests.

New presidential elections held in May 2014 brought military chief Abdel Fattah al-Sisi to the presidency. Under al-Sisi, new laws limiting basic freedoms were passed. More than 40,000 protesters were arrested between July 2013 and February 2015. Many were tortured and abused. The Muslim Brotherhood was outlawed, and hundreds of Muslim Brotherhood supporters were sentenced to

death for their role in violent protests. Despite a return to many of the conditions they had once fought to overthrow, many Egyptians approved of the new regime. They felt the tough policies were needed to fight the ever more violent Islamist movements in Egypt's Sinai Peninsula. "There is a time and place for human rights, but this is not it," said Cairo resident Khaled Abdelhamid. "How can we fight this [Islamist] terror if we do not stand behind our president?"

Meanwhile, in Yemen, a new government headed by president Abdu Rabbu Mansour Hadi took over in February 2012. Many people were unhappy with Hadi's performance, however. In September 2014, the Houthi—a Shia group from northern Yemen—took over the capital. With support from loyalists of ousted dictator Saleh, the Houthi demanded more say in the government. In January 2015, they placed Hadi and other key officials under house arrest,

Armed with antiaircraft guns, Libya Dawn seized control of Tripoli International Airport in August 2014.

forcing the president to resign. By April 2015, as Hadi's supporters squared off against the Houthi, the country had slid into civil war.

In Libya, the civil war that had ended in October 2011 with the killing of Muammar Gaddafi left the country fragmented. A new government called the National Transitional Council (NTC) tried to restore order. But people across the country divided along regional, tribal, and ethnic lines. Within 4 months, more than 300 **militia** groups had formed. Each group fought rival groups as well as the NTC. In June 2014, after Islamist political parties suffered defeats in parliamentary elections, civil war again split the country. This time the war was between supporters of Libya's official government and an Islamist militia called Libya Dawn. As the militia set up in the western part of the country, the official government fled to the east. Each side set up its own prime minister, parliament, and army. Thousands of citizens were killed or displaced in the ensuing battles. In January 2015, the United Nations (UN) began a series of peace talks. Many hoped the talks would bring an end to the war and help the country finally establish a democratic government.

By 2015, Syria had been locked in its own civil war for four years—ever since the uprising against Assad in 2011. Over time, the war evolved into a **sectarian** battle between the country's

Sunni majority and the Shia minority sect known as Alawite (to which Syrian president Assad belonged). By 2015, nearly 200,000 Syrians had died. Another 11 million had fled their homes. Many sought safety in Jordan, Lebanon, and Turkey. According to reports from U.S. spy agencies, Assad used chemical weapons against Sunni rebels in the Syrian capital of Damascus. An estimated 1,500 people were killed. "We're just living on the edge of life," said Syrian resident Mariam Akash. "We're always nervous, we're always afraid." Western powers were hesitant to assist the fractured rebel movement. But in 2013, the U.S. began training and arming small groups of Syrian rebels. As the war raged on, terrorist groups moved into the country, adding to its chaos.

In Bahrain, where protest movements were quickly put down in 2011, instability continued as well. Smaller protests rocked the country through early 2015. Most were broken up by police officers armed with tear gas and birdshot. Protesters often struck back with **Molotov cocktails**. In February 2014, Bahrain's king made it illegal to "[offend] publically the Monarch of the Kingdom of Bahrain." Doing so would result in jail time. In January 2015, citizenship was revoked for 72 Bahraini journalists, bloggers, and activists who had critiqued the government.

Millions of Syrians fled to refugee camps in Turkey while seeking asylum in nearby European countries.

CHAPTER FOUR

WORLDWIDE IMPACT

Angela Merkel

The effects of the Arab Spring were felt not only in the Middle East but also around the world. For the most part, Western leaders were verbally supportive of Arab democracy movements. After Egyptian dictator Mubarak resigned in February 2011, German chancellor Angela Merkel offered her congratulations to Egyptian citizens. "Today is a day of great joy," she said. "We are all witness to historic change. I share the joy of people on the streets of Egypt." The royal council of Qatar supported the removal of Mubarak as well. They declared it "a positive, important step towards the Egyptian people's aspirations of achieving democracy and reform and a life of dignity."

On May 19, 2011, only months after the start of the Arab Spring, President Obama delivered a speech supporting Middle Eastern democracy movements. "We face a historic opportunity," he said. "We have the chance to show that America values the dignity of the street vendor in Tunisia more than the raw power of the dictator. There must be no doubt that the United States of America welcomes change that advances self-determination and opportunity.

Although Libyan rebels were encouraged by Obama's speech, they were more relieved to receive military support from NATO a few months later.

Yes, there will be perils that accompany this moment of promise. But after decades of accepting the world as it is in the region, we have a chance to pursue the world as it should be…. We cannot hesitate to stand squarely on the side of those who are reaching for their rights." Despite such moral support, the U.S. and other Western countries were unwilling to involve themselves directly in most conflicts, with the notable exception of Libya. As violence escalated throughout the region, the U.S. and other countries closed their **embassies** in the war-torn nations of Syria, Libya, and Yemen.

Some countries were also concerned about the long-term effects of the Arab Spring on

POINTING OUT

DEFECTING FROM THE REGIME

*As Libyan dictator Muammar Gaddafi ordered his troops to fire on protesters, several members of his regime resigned. Some, such as General Abdel Fattah Younes al-Abidi, joined the rebels. Libya's **ambassador** to the UN also turned over his post. The protesters "did not throw a single stone and they were killed," he said. "I tell my brother Gadaffi: leave the Libyans alone." Ali Aujali, Libyan ambassador to the U.S., resigned as well. But he pledged his support to the Libyan people. "They need me to be around to get the international community to … stop this massacre," he said.*

Shortly before the civil war in Yemen began, Americans and others destroyed weapons and documents at their embassies.

important alliances. They feared that new leaders might turn Arab states that had once been allies of the West into enemies. Israel, in particular, feared renewed Arab–Israeli conflict. Leaders there especially worried that Arab nations such as Egypt and Jordan (with which Israel had been on good terms) might turn against it. Outside the Arab world, disagreements over how to deal with Syria caused tension in U.S.–Russian relations.

Within the region, the ongoing conflict led to changes in several alliances. Saudi Arabia had long been on poor terms with Qatar and Turkey. But in May 2015, the three nations formed an alliance to support Syrian rebels in that country's civil war. In Libya, however, Qatar and Turkey supported the Libya Dawn militia, while the Saudis backed the country's official government. And in Yemen, the Saudis backed the regime, while Iran supported the Houthi.

For most of the world, the biggest threat arising from the Arab Spring was the growth of the radical Islamist terrorist group that called itself the Islamic State of Iraq and Syria (ISIS). Formerly a part of the al Qaeda terrorist network in Iraq, ISIS broke off in 2013. Chaos and civil war in the region enabled the group to take over large portions of northern Iraq and Syria. It also made inroads into Libya and other Middle Eastern nations. In June 2014, ISIS declared a new caliphate—an Islamist government to rule over all Muslims worldwide.

POINTING OUT

HOSTAGE SITUATION

In November 2012, American journalist James Foley was captured by ISIS. The organization demanded a $132-million ransom for Foley's safe return. But U.S. policy prohibits negotiating with terrorists. Although U.S. forces later tried to mount a rescue, they were unsuccessful. In August 2014, ISIS posted a video of Foley's beheading. Since then, dozens more hostages from the U.S., Great Britain, Japan, and Jordan have been executed. Other countries, such as France, Spain, and Italy, have met ransom demands, and their prisoners have been released. However, according to CNN analyst Peter Bergen, "Every time a ransom is paid it increases the chance that other hostages will be taken."

By early 2015, nearly 10 million people fell under ISIS's direct rule. Within its territory, ISIS banned alcohol, cigarettes, and football. Women were required to cover themselves completely and to wear gloves and double-layered veils. Those who disobeyed faced severe punishment. The hands of thieves were chopped off, for example. Outsiders were not welcome in the region. Journalists and aid workers who ventured near were often kidnapped and beheaded.

Although ISIS was viewed with fear by many in both the Arab world and the West, others supported the movement. Young men from

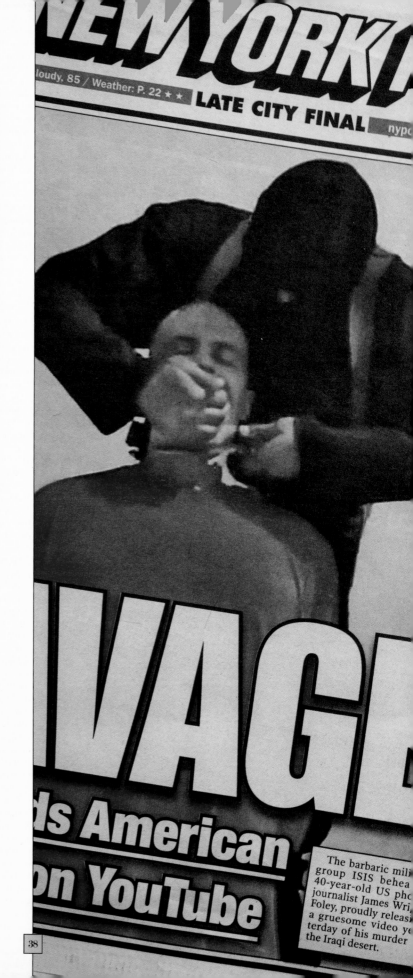

DAILY NEWS

- NYDailyNews.com

NEW YORK'S HOMETOWN NEWSPA

ISIS monsters behead U.S. journalist, taunt Obama over air strikes in Iraq

A DAY after threatening to "drown all (Americans) in blood," vile ISIS terrorists beheaded U.S. photojournalist James Foley (inset and r.) in a video they released Tuesday.

The barbaric bastards forced the handcuffed Foley – who was kidnapped in Syria two years ago – to read a statement condemning President Obama's successful air strikes on ISIS thugs in Iraq.

PAGES 4-6

Foley's death was widely covered in the press, and his executioner was later killed in an American drone strike.

SAVAGES

The Islamist ominously Message to Ar appeared Tube before kly taken down

PAGES 4-5

In 2014, ISIS supporters welcomed fighters and celebrated the new caliphate with a parade in northern Syria.

Tunisia, Yemen, and other Arab Spring countries flocked to ISIS-controlled lands to take up the black flag of the Islamic State. "The Islamic State is a true caliphate, a system that is fair and just, where you don't have to follow somebody's orders because he is rich or powerful. It is action, not theory," said one young ISIS supporter in Tunisia. "Democracy doesn't exist," said another ISIS fighter. "Do you think you are free?... The West is ruled by banks, not by parliaments…. Islam will get to you and bring you freedom."

In the fall of 2014, the U.S. began military operations against ISIS. In February 2015, Obama asked Congress to formally authorize air strikes against the Islamic State. "Now, make no mistake, this is a difficult mission, and it will remain difficult for some time," Obama said. The military's "core objective" was simple: destroy ISIS. The U.S. was joined by both traditional allies (such as Egypt, Saudi Arabia, and Jordan) and traditional enemies (including Iran, Syria, and Russia) in its opposition to ISIS.

Although the Arab Spring brought chaos to the Middle East, it also had some positive effects. According to some political analysts, the revolts taught Arab citizens the value of political participation. In addition, Arab regimes learned that violence against their own people could lead to their overthrow. Some observers believed the greatest beneficiaries of the Arab Spring would be women, who traditionally have few rights in Arab countries. As women fought alongside men during the Arab Spring, they may have been empowered to seek greater independence for themselves. "The biggest lesson women learned was the … self-confidence that comes from experience," said Natana DeLong-Bas, a professor of comparative theology at Boston College. "[This] planted the seeds that will continue to grow into demands for women's rights."

Ultimately, the long-term results of the Arab Spring remain uncertain. In the months immediately following the 2011 uprisings, political analysts were optimistic. But Marc Lynch says they "understated the risk of state failure and overstated the possibility of democratic consensus [agreement]." Still, as many countries returned to repressive measures, he noted that the people who had risen up against **authoritarian** governments once could do so again. James Gelvin, a professor of Middle Eastern history, agreed that there was no way to know what would happen next—and how change would affect the region. "As time goes on," he said, "events in one or more of the states … may force us to rethink the entire wave of uprisings." As political scientist Mark Haas and Middle East historian David Lesch noted, "Only time will tell if the Arab Spring will mark the beginning of a '[new] wave' of democratization." But whatever the outcome, nearly everyone agreed that the Arab Spring marked a definitive turning point in the Middle East.

Even after the Arab Spring, Arab women are in the political minority, as many countries do not grant them the same rights as men.

TIMELINE

December 17, 2010 — Tunisian fruit vendor Mohamed Bouazizi lights himself on fire, setting off protests through the country and beginning the Arab Spring.

January 14, 2011 — After the army refuses to fire on protesters, Tunisia's Zine el-Abidine Ben Ali resigns and flees the country.

February 11, 2011 — After widespread protests, president Hosni Mubarak resigns.

February 14, 2011 — Protests break out in Bahrain but are put down by the Saudi army a month later.

February 15, 2011 — Protests in Libya are met with force, sending the country into civil war.

March 2011 — Syrian schoolchildren are arrested for anti-regime graffiti, sparking protests that lead to a civil war.

August 2011 — With the help of a NATO campaign, Libyan rebels overthrow Muammar Gaddafi; Gaddafi is killed two months later.

November 2011 — Yemeni dictator Ali Abdullah Saleh resigns after being injured in a bomb blast.

June 2012 — Mohamed Morsi of the Islamist Muslim Brotherhood movement is elected Egyptian president but is ousted by the army a year later.

September 2013 — The U.S. begins providing weapons to Syrian rebels.

May 2014 — Egyptian military chief Abdel Fattah al-Sisi is elected president and institutes new authoritarian laws.

June 2014 — Renewed civil war breaks out in Libya.

August 2014 — The U.S. begins launching air strikes against ISIS.

December 2014 — Tunisia elects Beji Caid Essebsi president, becoming the first Arab Spring country to establish a successful democracy.

January 2015 — Yemen's president Abdu Rabbu Mansour Hadi resigns after being placed under house arrest by the Shia Houthi group.

ambassador—an official who represents his or her government in another nation

authoritarian—characterized by a requirement for absolute obedience to a leader, without individual rights and freedoms

censored—blocked or deleted information from newspaper articles, books, movies, or other sources, often for political or moral reasons

communist—involving a system of government in which all property and business is owned and controlled by the state, with the goal of creating a classless society

constitutional—having to do with the system of laws and principles that defines how a specific government or institution functions

coups—uprisings in which one person or group takes power from another, often by force

democratic—part of a democracy, a form of government in which the people rule either directly or by electing representatives to rule on their behalf

dictators—rulers with complete power, who often rule by force

dynasties—series of rulers from the same family

embassies—offices of government officials who are stationed in a foreign country

human rights—basic rights considered to belong to all people, including life, equality, and freedom of thought and expression

imports—goods that have been brought into one country from another, usually for sale

interim—serving temporarily between two time periods such as the fall of one government and the establishment of a new one

militia—groups of citizens who band together to form their own army, often to fight the government

Molotov cocktails—homemade bombs consisting of a bottle filled with gasoline and a rag that is lit before the bomb is thrown at a target

monarchies—governments led by kings or queens

North Atlantic Treaty Organization (NATO)—a military alliance between the U.S., Canada, and several European nations

Ottoman Empire—an empire that ruled over much of southeastern Europe, the Middle East, and North Africa from the 1300s until 1922

Ramadan—the Islamic holy month during which Muslims fast daily—they do not eat from sunrise to sunset

regime—the rule of a specific government or leader, usually oppressive

sectarian—marked by disagreements among different religious groups or sects

whistleblower—someone who exposes wrongdoing within an organization or government for the purpose of stopping it

Gause, F. Gregory III. "Why Middle East Studies Missed the Arab Spring: The Myth of Authoritarian Stability." *Foreign Affairs*. July/August 2011. http://www.foreignaffairs.com/articles/67932/f-gregory-gause-iii/why -middle-east-studies-missed-the-arab-spring.

Gelvin, James L. *The Arab Uprisings: What Everyone Needs to Know*. New York: Oxford University Press, 2012.

Haas, Mark L., and David W. Lesch, eds. *The Arab Spring: Change and Resistance in the Middle East*. Boulder, Colo.: Westview, 2012.

Kirkpatrick, David D. "New Freedoms in Tunisia Drive Support for ISIS." *The New York Times*, October 21, 2014. http://www.nytimes.com/2014 /10/22/world/africa/new-freedoms-in-tunisia-drive-support-for-isis.html

Loveluck, Louisa. "The Price of Egypt's Economic Recovery: Police Brutality, Torture and a Strangled Press." *The Spectator*, February 4, 2015. http://blogs .spectator.co.uk/coffeehouse/2015/02/egypt/.

Lynch, Marc. *The Arab Uprising: The Unfinished Revolutions of the New Middle East*. New York: Public Affairs, 2012.

Noueihed, Lin. "Peddler's Martyrdom Launched Tunisia's Revolution." *Reuters*, January 19, 2011. http://www.reuters.com/article/2011/01/19 /tunisia-protests-bouazizi-idAFLDE70G18J20110119.

Wehrey, Frederic. "Libya's War-Weary Make Peace?" *Foreign Affairs*, February 2, 2015. http://www.foreignaffairs.com/features/letters-from /libyas-war-weary-make-peace.

Arab Spring: An Interactive Timeline of the Middle East Protests
http://www.theguardian.com/world/interactive
/2011/mar/22/middle-east-protest-interactive-timeline
This site tracks all the major events of the
Arab Spring throughout the Middle East.

Scholastic: Unrest in the Middle East
http://www.scholastic.com/browse/collection.jsp?id=816
Images, maps, and background information
help explain the events of the Arab Spring.

Note: Every effort has been made to ensure that the websites listed above are suitable for children, that they have educational value, and that they contain no inappropriate material. However, because of the nature of the Internet, it is impossible to guarantee that these sites will remain active indefinitely or that their contents will not be altered.

INDEX